GOD IS GOOD, AND SO ARE YOU

A Child's Guide to Spirituality

written by
Jim Krauel

illustrated by
Aria Jones

God is Good and So Are You: A Child's Guide to Spirituality
Copyright © 2020 by Jim Krauel

All rights reserved. This book or any portion thereof may not be reproduced or used in any manner whatsoever without the express written permission of the publisher, except for the use of brief quotations in a book review.

Printed in the United States of America

Illustrations by Aria Jones
Cover and Interior Layout by Claire Flint Last

Luminare Press
442 Charnelton St.
Eugene, OR 97401
www.luminarepress.com

LCCN: 2020903842
ISBN: 978-1-64388-198-0

Dedicated to
Calvin, Jules, Lucy, Pilar and Sofia.
May you Always be filled with Love.

Special thanks to Anna and Jack
for sharing their wisdom.

God is Good and so are You. Sometimes, it's really hard for kids to believe this because things in life don't always feel good, but it's really true. God never promised that there wouldn't be problems in life, but He did promise to be with you during the good times and the bad. That's the amazing part. He sits with you when you are having a great day and He sits with you when you're having a bad day. He is always with you. That's what this book is about.

We will show you some of the great things that have been said about children by some fabulous people, and how important and special you are no matter where you live, how big you are, or what color skin you have.

Helen Keller was born in America about 100 years ago. When she was a little girl she lost her ability to see and hear, but she still became one of the smartest people ever. She loved God and children very much. She understood that God didn't cause her to lose her eyesight and her hearing, but that He helped her deal with it.

Helen Keller

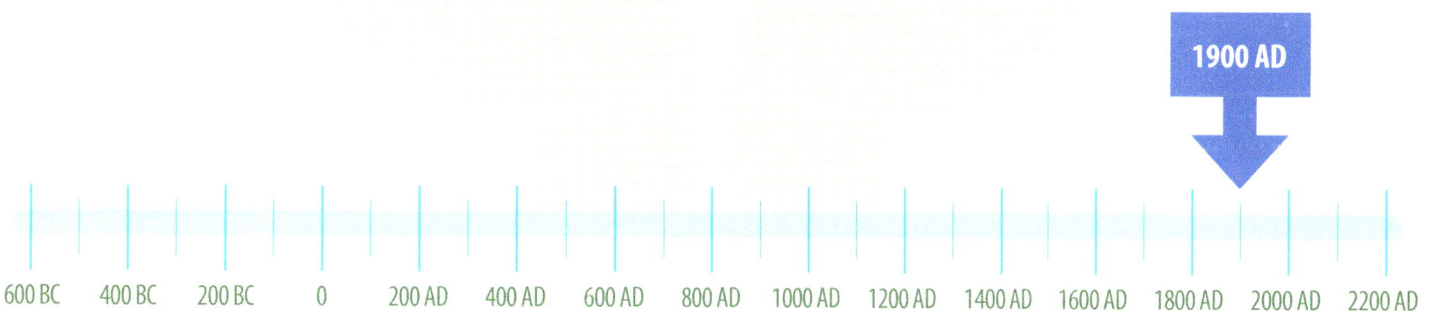

In this quote, Helen Keller is saying that children are better able to make friends with God than adults are, and that if you have a friendship with God, you can overcome any problem in your life.

(Mark 10:13) "And they were bringing children to Him so that He might touch them; but the disciples blocked them. When Jesus saw this, He was upset and said, "Let the children to come to Me; do not hinder them; for the kingdom of God belongs to kids such as these."

This quote comes from the New Testament in the Bible. It's from a man named Mark who was talking about Jesus Christ. Jesus lived in Jerusalem about 2000 years ago. Jesus loved children. All of them. It didn't matter if it was a boy or a girl, or what part of town they lived in, or what their body type was. Jesus just loved them as they were.

Jesus

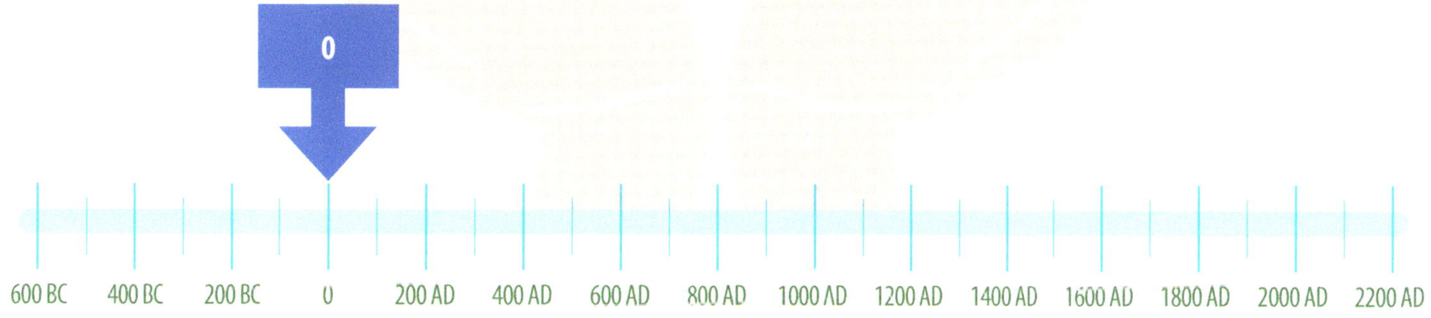

600 BC   400 BC   200 BC   0   200 AD   400 AD   600 AD   800 AD   1000 AD   1200 AD   1400 AD   1600 AD   1800 AD   2000 AD   2200 AD

What happened in this story is that the religious leaders tried to keep the kids away from Jesus. He didn't like this. The hard-hearted religious people were confused. They were confused because they didn't realize how important kids are. Some adults are still like that today. They think kids get in the way when the adults are trying to do things. According to Jesus, the kids are the ones that should be teaching the adults how to act. This is true because kids live in their hearts better than adults. So, whenever you get a chance, teach adults how to love people the right way.

"A truly great man never puts away the simplicity of a child."
—**Confucius**

Confucius lived a long time ago, about 500 years before Jesus. History regards him as one of the wisest men that has ever lived. He said many wonderful things that people still try to follow and learn from today.

Confucius

500 BC

600 BC   400 BC   200 BC   0   200 AD   400 AD   600 AD   800 AD   1000 AD   1200 AD   1400 AD   1600 AD   1800 AD   2000 AD   2200 AD

In this quote about children, Confucius is saying that if you really want to be a truly great man when you grow up, you need to hang on to the simple parts of being a child. What this means is that when we grow up we sometimes make things messy and complicated. We forget that true love is simple. Kids understand this better than adults.

"To me nothing in the world is as precious as a genuine smile, especially from a child."
—Jalāl ad-Dīn Muḥammad Balkhi (Rumi)

Jalāl ad-Dīn Muḥammad Balkhi is also known as Rumi. Rumi was a man that truly loved God. He was a writer and a poet that lived about 1000 years after Jesus. He wrote many stories about how wonderful and beautiful God is. And if you asked him to describe God, he would say "God is Love."

Rumi

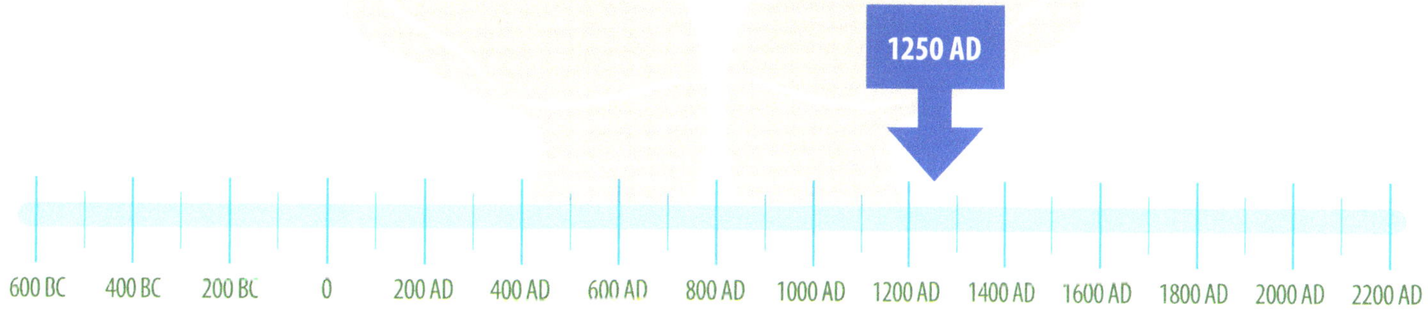

1250 AD

600 BC 400 BC 200 BC 0 200 AD 400 AD 600 AD 800 AD 1000 AD 1200 AD 1400 AD 1600 AD 1800 AD 2000 AD 2200 AD

In this quote, Rumi is saying that real smiles from people are special because they are natural and pure. It's interesting that he added the part that says, "Especially from a child." Why do you think such a wise man would add that part? I think I know. I think it's because he, like Jesus, knew that kids are very special and that things that come from kids are even better than things that come from adults. Rumi was a very smart man and he had a great relationship with God. He knew that a real smile from a child is the most precious thing in the world.

Martin Luther King Jr. loved God and children very much. He lived about 75 years ago. He spent his whole life trying to make people realize that ALL children are created equally. He knew that God doesn't care what color your skin is, so he tried to share that wisdom with the world.

Martin Luther King Jr.

1950 AD

600 BC 400 BC 200 BC 0 200 AD 400 AD 600 AD 800 AD 1000 AD 1200 AD 1400 AD 1600 AD 1800 AD 2000 AD 2200 AD

In this quote, Martin Luther King Jr. is saying that love is the key to everything in life. It's the magic force that connects all of us to each other. Of course this is true, but sometimes adults forget how true it really is. Kids can help adults remember this.

Anne Frank lived about the same time as Martin Luther King Jr., but in a different part of the world. Like Martin Luther King Jr., she saw people suffer, but she was so in touch with God that she knew that God was with her when she was lonely or afraid.

Anne Frank

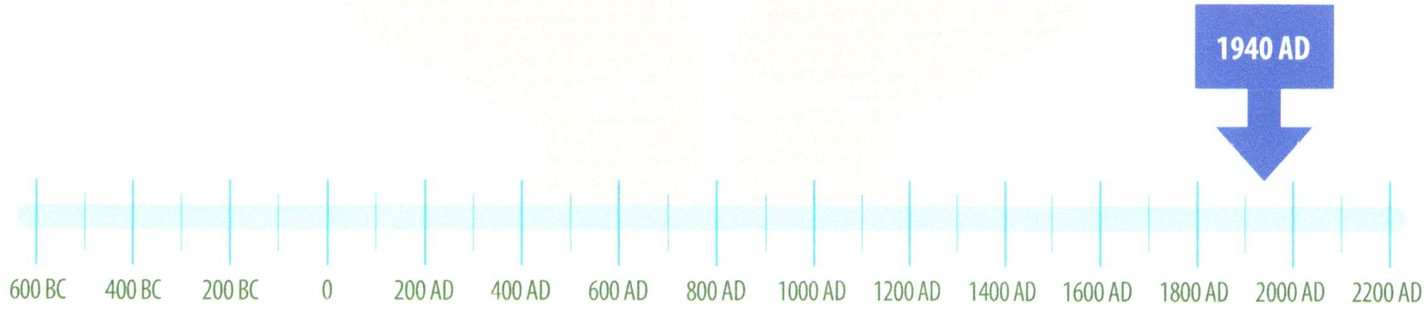

1940 AD

600 BC 400 BC 200 BC 0 200 AD 400 AD 600 AD 800 AD 1000 AD 1200 AD 1400 AD 1600 AD 1800 AD 2000 AD 2200 AD

Even though she was only 13 years old when she wrote this, Anne knew that one of the very best places to find God is in nature. This is true for you too. If you are feeling alone or afraid, try to take a look at the stars or smell a pretty flower. It really works!

Nelson Mandela said this only 20 years ago. He lived in South Africa and he loved children and God very much. He went through many struggles, but he kept a cheerful attitude and he changed the world with his pursuit of truth and justice.

Nelson Mandela

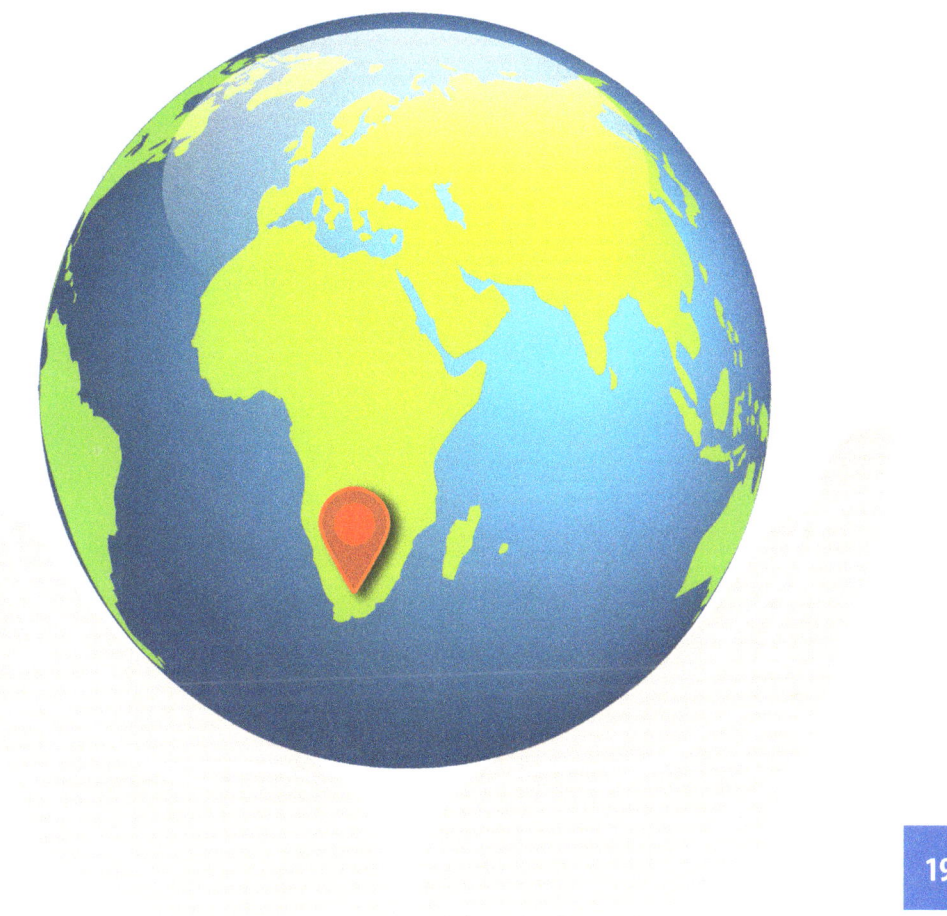

1990 AD

600 BC 400 BC 200 BC 0 200 AD 400 AD 600 AD 800 AD 1000 AD 1200 AD 1400 AD 1600 AD 1800 AD 2000 AD 2200 AD

What Nelson Mandela is saying in this quote is that adults made him feel worn out, but spending time with kids always managed to make him feel better and stronger. Kids are always really good at making adults feel better if they are given a chance. Some adults realize this, but many do not.

Kahlil Gibran lived about the same time as Anne Frank, but he lived in a different part of the world. He wrote many famous books that have been read by people all over the entire world. He loved God very much and he was a very smart person.

Kahlil Gibran

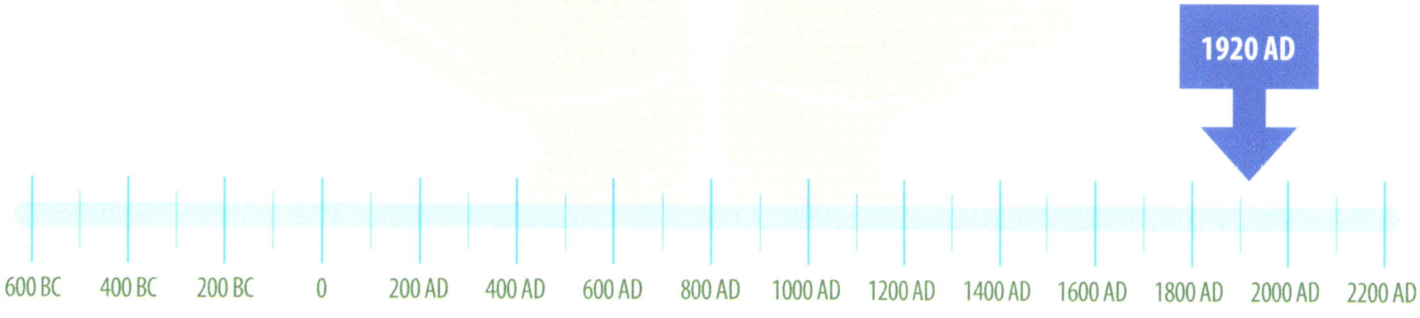

1920 AD

600 BC   400 BC   200 BC   0   200 AD   400 AD   600 AD   800 AD   1000 AD   1200 AD   1400 AD   1600 AD   1800 AD   2000 AD   2200 AD

In this quote, Kahlil Gibran is saying that it's good to cry and it's good to laugh and that we should all bow before children. That means that adults need to do a better job of understanding how valuable kids are. Sometimes adults get too busy and worried about silly things and forget how much God loves children. Kahlil Gibran is reminding us that since God loves children so much, so should adults.

"Do not grow old, no matter how long you live. Never cease to stand like curious children before the Great Mystery into which we were born."
—Albert Einstein

Albert Einstein lived about the same time as Martin Luther King Jr. Most people think that he was the smartest man that ever lived. Even though he was really, really smart, Albert Einstein knew that only God knows all the secrets to the universe.

Albert Einstein

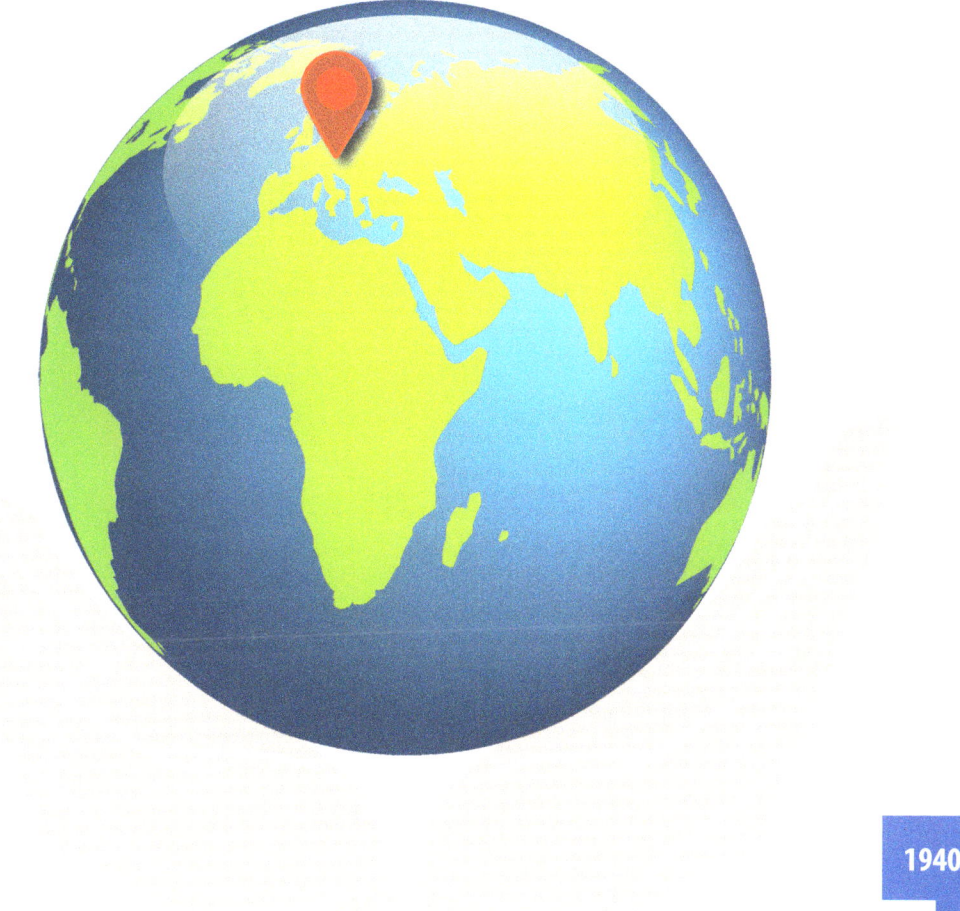

1940 AD

600 BC   400 BC   200 BC   0   200 AD   400 AD   600 AD   800 AD   1000 AD   1200 AD   1400 AD   1600 AD   1800 AD   2000 AD   2200 AD

In this quote, Albert Einstein is saying that adults should try to live their lives like kids and not grow old. Of course our bodies are going to get old, but he is teaching us to never let our hearts and our spirits get old.

Walt Disney lived in America. He lived about the same time as Albert Einstein. He is the man who invented and built Disneyland. He loved God very much and he really, really, really loved kids.

Walt Disney

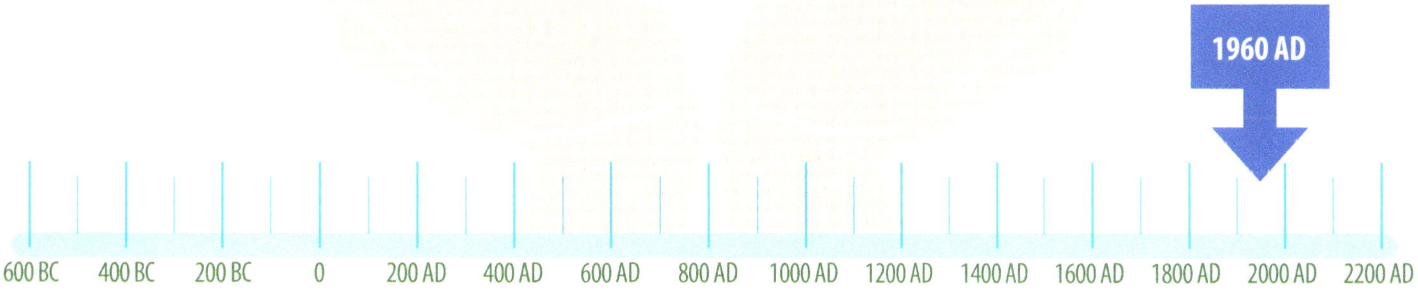

1960 AD

600 BC 400 BC 200 BC 0 200 AD 400 AD 600 AD 800 AD 1000 AD 1200 AD 1400 AD 1600 AD 1800 AD 2000 AD 2200 AD

In this quote, Walt Disney is trying to remind us that we should all try to be like children. He is saying that kids are great, but sometimes they forget about their beauty and value when they start becoming adults. Some adults get distracted by the world. We all need to do a better job of remembering what really matters in life.

Muhammad Ali lived just a short time ago, about the same time as Walt Disney. He is the greatest boxer of all time. He loved God and kids very much.

Muhammad Ali

1980 AD

600 BC   400 BC   200 BC   0   200 AD   400 AD   600 AD   800 AD   1000 AD   1200 AD   1400 AD   1600 AD   1800 AD   2000 AD   2200 AD

In this quote, Muhammad Ali is saying that he didn't realize how great kids are until he was older, and he wishes he had figured this out earlier in his life. Kids truly are amazing and he is encouraging all adults to figure this out as soon as possible.

"The warrior is one who sacrifices himself for the good of others. His task is to take care of the elderly, the defenseless, and above all, the children, the future of humanity."
—Sitting Bull

Sitting Bull was a great Native American Chief. He was a very, very wise man. He lived in America about the same time as Kahlil Gibran. He loved God and children very much.

Sitting Bull

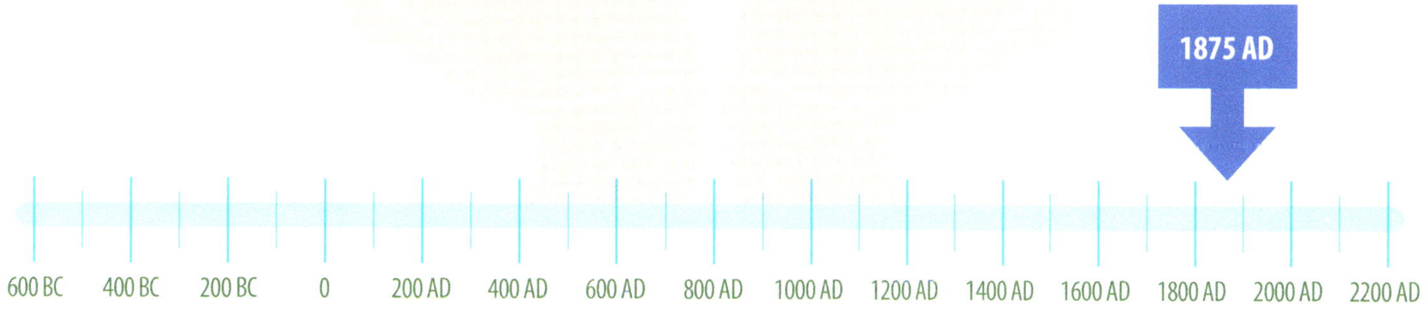

1875 AD

600 BC 400 BC 200 BC 0 200 AD 400 AD 600 AD 800 AD 1000 AD 1200 AD 1400 AD 1600 AD 1800 AD 2000 AD 2200 AD

In this quote, Sitting Bull is telling us that the people who are truly strong are not the bullies and tough guys. No, he is saying that truly strong people use their strength to take care of other people, especially children.

Fred Rogers had a famous TV show called Mister Rogers' Neighborhood. It was a show for kids about God and Love. It was on for many years and millions of kids watched it. The show taught us that we should Love everyone no matter what they look like because God Loves everyone no matter what they look like.

Fred Rogers

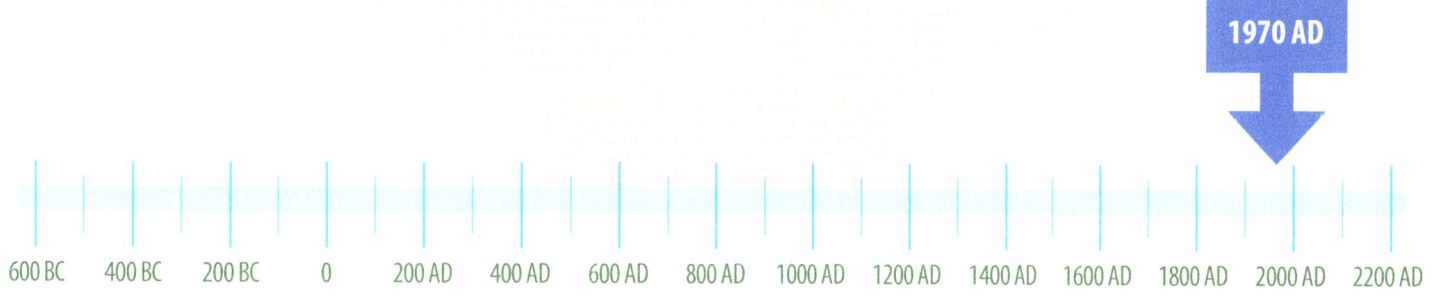

In this quote, Mister Rogers is showing us how much he values children and those people that help children. This is a wonderful message that all adults should learn. Mister Rogers loved God very much and he dedicated his life to spread that love to kids around the world. He lived about the same time as Muhammad Ali.

"We need to see each child as a gift to be welcomed, cherished, and protected."
—**Pope Francis**

Pope Francis is still alive. He lives in Italy now, but he is from Argentina. He loves God very much. He also loves all children.

Pope Francis

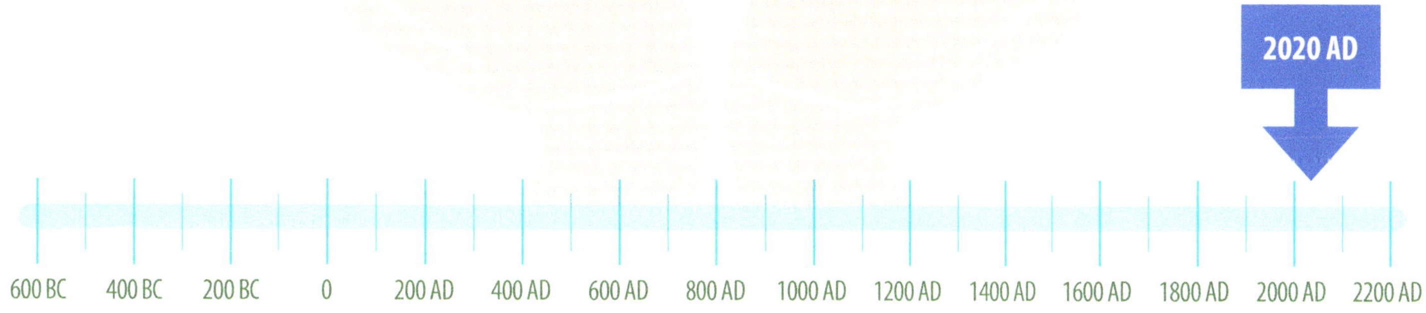

2020 AD

600 BC 400 BC 200 BC 0 200 AD 400 AD 600 AD 800 AD 1000 AD 1200 AD 1400 AD 1600 AD 1800 AD 2000 AD 2200 AD

In this quote, Pope Francis is saying that in God's eyes, all children are the same. They should be welcomed at all times; they all should be loved and they all should be taken care of. It's important for kids to realize that God doesn't care how big your house is or how smart you are or how tall you are. He just wants you to feel loved.

Like Pope Francis, the Dalai Lama is still alive today. If you look at his picture you'll see how happy he looks. The reason he's so happy is because he loves God and he knows that God is Love.

The Dalai Lama

2020 AD

600 BC 400 BC 200 BC 0 200 AD 400 AD 600 AD 800 AD 1000 AD 1200 AD 1400 AD 1600 AD 1800 AD 2000 AD 2200 AD

In this quote, the Dalai Lama is saying that parents should pay close attention to what they teach kids. Instead of always teaching them math, science, and reading, he is saying that parents should teach their kids how to Love with their hearts. Don't be afraid to remind your parents about this the next time they are doing Flash Cards with you!

C.S. Lewis lived in England. He lived about the same time as Nelson Mandela. He has written many books that have inspired people all over the entire world. Some of his books are as popular today as they were 50 years ago. C.S. Lewis loved God and children.

C.S. Lewis

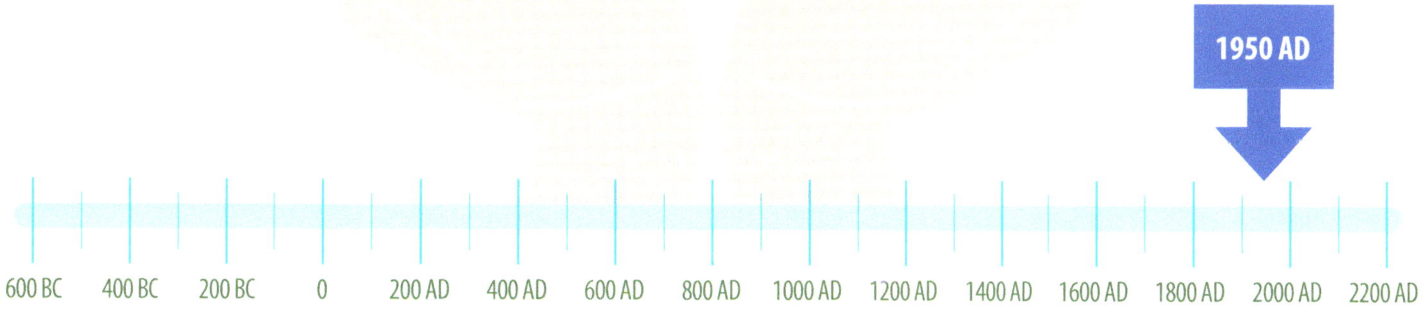

1950 AD

600 BC   400 BC   200 BC   0   200 AD   400 AD   600 AD   800 AD   1000 AD   1200 AD   1400 AD   1600 AD   1800 AD   2000 AD   2200 AD

In this quote, C.S. Lewis is warning adults not to think that their jobs are more important than their kids. Some parents get busy with their lives and jobs and need to be reminded that there is nothing more important than children.

Pocahontas lived about 500 years ago. She lived in America and then moved to England. She loved God very much and she was one of the strongest, most courageous women of that era. She set a great example for children back then and for children today.

Pocahontas

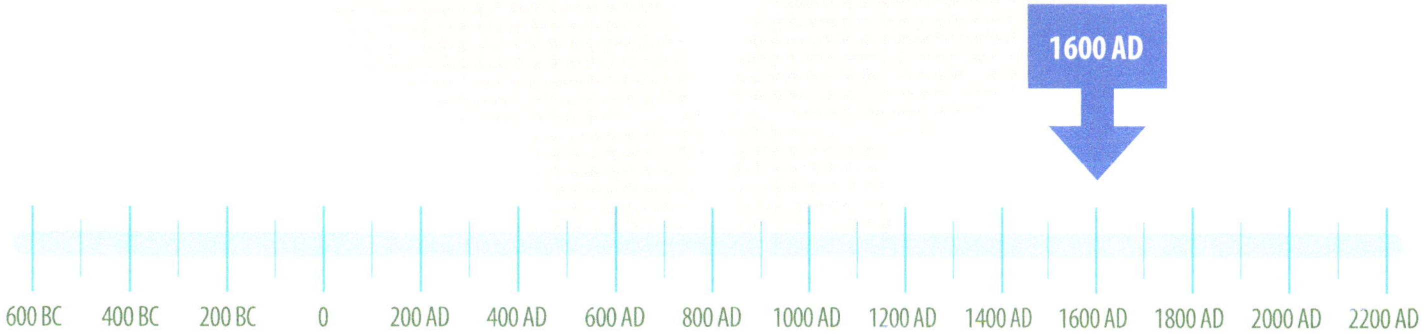

1600 AD

600 BC 400 BC 200 BC 0 200 AD 400 AD 600 AD 800 AD 1000 AD 1200 AD 1400 AD 1600 AD 1800 AD 2000 AD 2200 AD

In this quote, Pocahontas is saying that inside every child there is a path. A path that leads to Love and to God. Some kids don't realize this. They think that they aren't good enough for Love and God. This isn't true. Pocahontas knew that some kids might worry that they aren't good enough so she gave us this beautiful message.

Isaac Newton lived about the same time as Pocahontas. He also lived in England. Many people think he is the best and smartest scientist of all time. He was very wise and he loved God very much.

Sir Isaac Newton

1650 AD

600 BC 400 BC 200 BC 0 200 AD 400 AD 600 AD 800 AD 1000 AD 1200 AD 1400 AD 1600 AD 1800 AD 2000 AD 2200 AD

What Sir Isaac Newton is saying here is that even though he was a brilliant man, he was wise enough to understand that there are many secrets that only God knows, and that there are millions of things that cannot be figured out. Instead of being frustrated about those secrets, he is telling us to enjoy the fact that there is so much undiscovered truth and beauty out there in the world.

"Old age is a hindrance to creativity, but cannot crush my youthful spirit."
—Rembrandt Harmenszoon van Rijn

This man was so smart, popular, and wise, that he is now known simply by his first name, Rembrandt. Most people consider him to be the greatest artist of all time. His art has been admired by millions of people for hundreds of years. He lived about 400 years ago, around the same time as Sir Isaac Newton. He loved God so much that he painted pictures using God as an inspiration.

Rembrandt

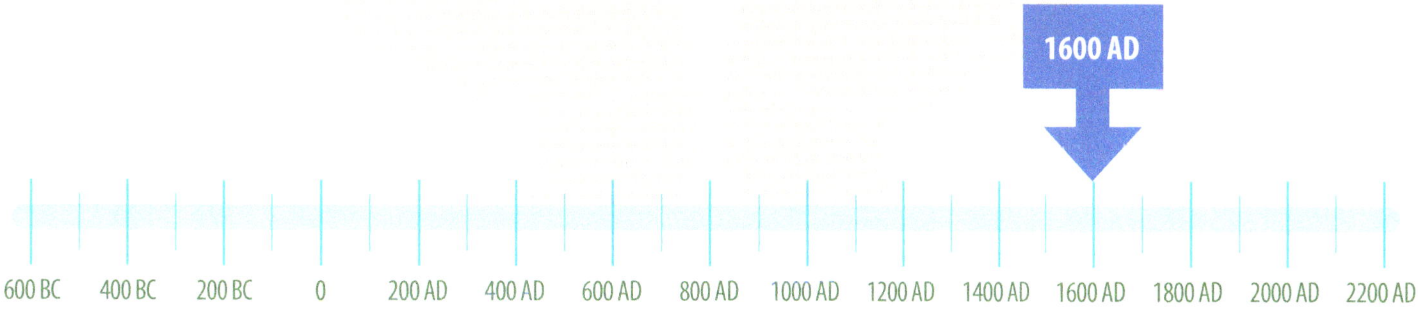

1600 AD

600 BC   400 BC   200 BC   0   200 AD   400 AD   600 AD   800 AD   1000 AD   1200 AD   1400 AD   1600 AD   1800 AD   2000 AD   2200 AD

In this quote, Rembrandt is saying that when we get older we can lose some physical gifts, but old age cannot take away the beauty of a child-like spirit. What he understood was that children have a very special spirit and they should try to keep that spirit alive in themselves as they grow older.

"Hold the hand of the child within you. For this child, nothing is impossible."
—Paulo Coelho

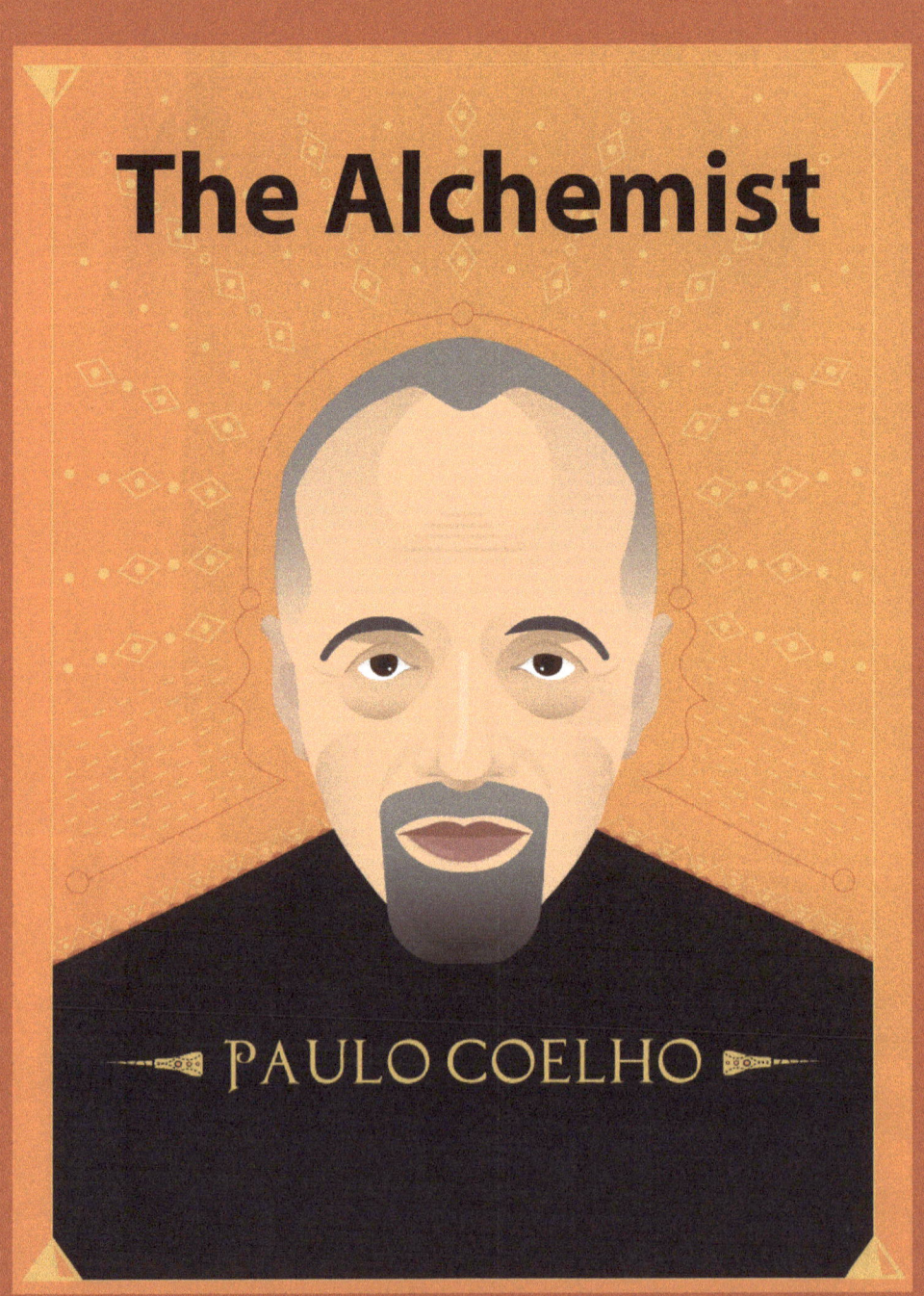

Paulo Coelho is still alive today. He lives in Brazil. He has written some incredible books that have been read by millions of people all over the world. He loves God and he loves kids.

Paulo Coelho

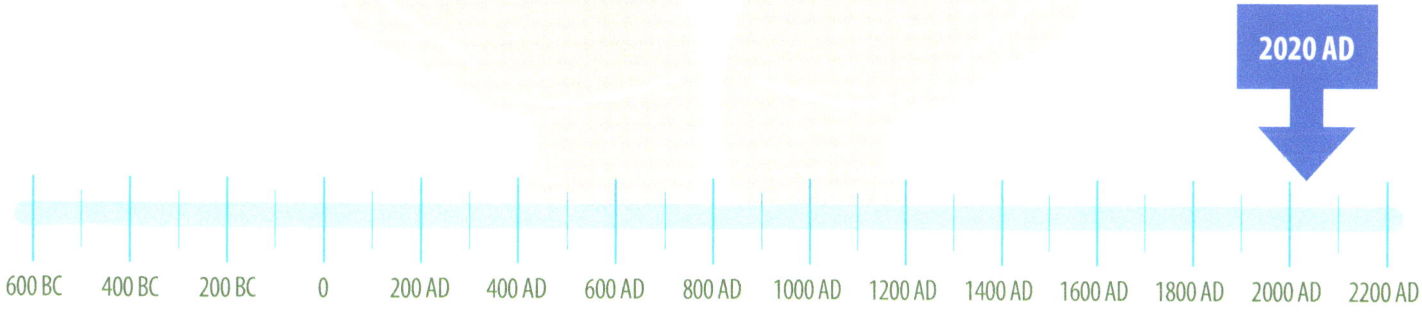

2020 AD

600 BC   400 BC   200 BC   0   200 AD   400 AD   600 AD   800 AD   1000 AD   1200 AD   1400 AD   1600 AD   1800 AD   2000 AD   2200 AD

In this quote, Paulo Coelho is helping us see that we all have a piece of God inside of us—even adults. He is encouraging us to search our hearts and embrace our inner child, because that is where God is. He knows that once we can do this, we will find that nothing is impossible.

Malala was born in Pakistan and now lives in England. She is only 20 years old, but she is very wise. She loves God very much and she loves children.

Malala Yousafzai

2020 AD

600 BC 400 BC 200 BC 0 200 AD 400 AD 600 AD 800 AD 1000 AD 1200 AD 1400 AD 1600 AD 1800 AD 2000 AD 2200 AD

In this quote, Malala is saying that the struggles she went through as a child are the same as other kids around the world. She is encouraging kids to be strong and courageous and to stand up for themselves.

All of the people you just read about are very different. They lived at different times in history. They all had different colored skin. Some were rich and some were poor. Some were tall and some were short. They lived in different places all over the world. They all knew the same thing though. Regardless of their differences, they each knew that God is Love.

They knew that God never made promises about life being easy, but that God did promise to be with all of us when things are scary and painful. They also knew that ALL children hold a very special place in God's heart. This is not just another silly thing that is made up by adults. Remember, these are some of the smartest and most amazing people in the whole wide world and they all agree on that.

Whenever life gets yucky and confusing, learn to look inside your own heart for answers because that's where God is. Sometimes, you might have to dig around a little bit, but you will find those answers. When you get sad or lonely, remember that everyone else feels the same way on certain days. Sometimes, when we are feeling bad, we start to think that we are the only person who has ever felt this way. The truth is that everyone who has ever lived has had days when they felt scared and alone.

The people you just read about in this book have had many of those kinds of days. Guess what they did? They searched their own hearts, they kept trusting God, and they kept on loving their friends and neighbors.

God is Good and So Are You is the title of this book, but it's more than that. It's a true promise that you can hold on to whenever life gets a little messy.

www.ingramcontent.com/pod-product-compliance
Lightning Source LLC
LaVergne TN
LVHW072050060526
838200LV00061B/4707